Beekeeping For Beginners:

Apiculture Basics

By

Timothy Tripp

ISBN-13: 978-1490574929

Table of Contents

Beekeeping For Beginners: Apiculture Basics

By Timothy Tripp

© Copyright 2013 Timothy Tripp

First Published, 2013

Printed in the United States of America

Introduction

Many people would like to make their own honey but think it's a very complicated, involved process. The truth is that beekeeping is a very simple undertaking and nearly anyone can learn to do it. It's a fascinating hobby that you can enjoy for years, spending very little of your own money but reaping enormous benefits.

Things to think about—what will you do with the honey? Is it a hobby or a business? Do you garden a lot? Don't use pesticides if you have bees. Your neighbors may be using them and you can try to bribe them to stop with the promise of honey. Farmers nearby won't stop but bees do build up a tolerance to certain chemicals.

Chapter 1. Begin With Hives

You can make your own hives or you can buy a commercially manufactured hive. The great thing about beekeeping is that you only need one hive to start with. Hives are fairly small and can be kept in your back yard. In fact, many suburban beekeepers can be involved in this hobby for years and no one even knows they have a hive!

There are two types of beehives, the Top Bar and the Langstroth and both are basically boxes with trays for the bees to work and live in. A Top Bar hive has trays that you pull up to get to the bees, harvest the honey, and perform maintenance tasks. Once the trays are full of honey they can be quite heavy and you'll need to be strong enough to lift them up and out of the hive. The Langstroth bee hives are a bit like a Top Bar on its side—the trays pull out parallel to the ground. Langstroth bee hives are easier to manage, particularly if you are a smaller person. Langstroth hives are popular among school aged children and beekeepers who have retired and are seeking in interesting hobby that doesn't take a lot of upper body strength.

Top Bar hives are easy to build if you want to build your own. The sloped sides of a Kenya style Top Bar makes the combs stronger and less likely to collapse when they become full of honey. However, this also means that the combs are not built on a strong foundation and may be attached awkwardly; there are no frames with which to build the comb on so you have to be careful about the way you handle the bars. You are also limited in the size of your hive unless you want to add another hive alongside the original. If you want more honey you'll have to harvest more frequently; Top Bar hives limit your harvesting methods to crushing and straining.

Langstroth hives are the type that you usually see when you spot a man made hive. They look like boxes and can be short or tall, depending on how large the colony it. If your bee colony grows you can simply add another hive atop the original without breaking up the colony as you would with a Top Bar hive. Harvesting and maintenance is much easier as all you have to do is pull out the drawers.

No matter what type of hive you choose, you should make sure that it is placed off the ground so that the bottom won't rot from moisture and it has sufficient drainage and air flow. Many people use concrete blocks for this purpose while others build a stand. Taking into account the nature of ground and how it settles, some beekeepers have even poured concrete foundations for their hives to minimize settling.

Chapter 2. Obtaining The Hives

There are many places you can get beehives and varying prices, too. One of the best ways to find good prices is to ask other, experienced beekeepers. They know which brands are poorly made and which are quality so that you can spend your money wisely. They know of people selling hives that have never been used, which can save you a bit of money.

You can get hives from local feed stores but they probably won't have them in stock. You can usually order them from a catalog; one advantage of buying hives this way is that the store may deliver it to your property as a courtesy.

There are many places online to buy beehives, too. An advantage of buying online is that you can research the company and see what its customers say about it on its site or, preferably, consumer comment sites. Online prices are often lower than your local store but if something goes wrong with the purchase you won't be able to resolve the problem face to face and may have to pay return shipping.

Buying used hives presents a significant savings but unless you want to take a chance on losing your bees you'll need to thoroughly clean and sterilize it before introducing your colony. Used bee hives can pass on disease, mites, and pests to new colonies unless they are well sterilized. Many novice beekeepers buy used hives from online auction sites; the sellers may claim they are free of disease and pests but if you go this route you should nevertheless clean them thoroughly yourself.

Chapter 3. Beekeeping Equipment

You don't need a lot of equipment to keep bees. Unlike other hobbies or businesses, all you basically need is some items to protect yourself from beestings and a few things to help you maintain the hives and harvest the honey.

You'll need a hooded suit or a suit and a veiled hat and gloves. Of course, you must wear closed-toed shoes to protect your feet. Some beekeepers don't wear any protective clothing but they are usually more experienced in the skills of beekeeping and know how to keep from alarming the bees. Bees do not sting out of malice but to protect their hive and their queen. Once you learn how to keep them calm you'll feel more comfortable around the hive but you should still wear protective clothing.

You will also need a smoker to make the bees calm down when you work with them. Smoke has been used for this purpose since bees were raised in ancient times but scientists have found that it actually masks the pheromones that raise alarms in the hive from the guard bees. Since there is no alarm raised, the bees continue to go about their business calmly. A smoker is small enough to hold in your hands and doesn't take much fuel; you can use paper, egg carton material, pine needles or wood in the fuel chamber.

Once you fire up a smoker it can last for several hours before needing replenishment. The fuel is kept in a small chamber where it smolders until you depress the bellows, blowing smoke from its spout. Many newer smokers come with a protective wire grid around the fuel chamber since it can get quite hot. Without this protection it can be a fire hazard or burn you if you get careless. Other smokers have safety guards around the fuel chamber. You can make your own smoker if you enjoy this type of activity and have the time but it's usually less costly to buy one. A basic smoker averages $25-$30.

There are also various hive tools, brushes, spacers, cleaning tools, knives and other paraphernalia you'll need to buy or make. You'll spend about $30-$100 dollars on all these tools that help you work safely with the hive and its bees.

You may be tempted to purchase used hives to save some money but be careful to sterilize them thoroughly so that your bees don't contract a disease or infection suffered by the previous residents. Langstroth is made of boxes stacked atop one another; you pull them out like drawers to get to the bees, do maintenance, and harvest the honey eventually. You can add boxes if your colony needs more space. A Top Bar hive is arranged horizontally and can be problematic for people who don't have a lot of upper body strength to pull them up and out.

Chapter 4. Choosing and Buying Your Bees

You should start with a small colony because by then end of a year your bees will have replaced themselves and more. By ordering a small colony you won't be facing overcrowding by the end of the honey-making season. A small colony of bees can cost as little as $70 or as much as $300 depending on the bees and the company you buy them from, called an Apiary.

Did you know that there are about 20,000 types of bees? Fortunately, you don't have to consider that many options! The Italian honeybee is considered the best for beginners. It's a common breed you'll find in many hives, whether they belong to novices or experts. They are very well suited to the climate in the U.S. and have a gentle temperament, rarely stinging without severe provocation. Italian honeybees breed even after they've finished making honey for the season so you'll have a very stable hive even in cold weather. You do have to feed them frequently in the winter but the colony grows quickly and they produce a good comb.

The Carnolian bee is also good for beginners and experts alike, a bee originating in the Alps of Austria and Yugoslavia. Although they are prone to swarming (which you can prevent with a smoker) they don't require as much food in the winter as the Italian honeybee. They build their colony quickly, produce excellent combs and have a gentle temperament despite their tendency to swarm when alarmed.

Another type of bee that is recommended for beginners is the Caucasian honeybee, one that originates in the Caucasian Mountains of the Black Sea. They adapt well to very cold winters but are well known for robbing other hives. Caucasian bees breed quickly and their tongues are exceptionally long, allowing them to gather more nectar for the honey making process. They tend to produce a lot of propolis (used to fill empty spaces in the comb) so beekeeping can be quite sticky. As for their temperament, they are generally very calm but once the hive is alarmed it can take quite some time to calm them down. You definitely need to develop good smoker skills if you decide to keep Caucasian bees.

Russian honeybees are a new, hybrid bee that was bred in Russia to resist varroa and tracheal mites. You will not have a problem with mites affecting your bees with this breed. They propagate quickly in the spring and are tolerant of harsh winters. However, they are quite costly and also very apt to swarm at very little provocation.

You may start with a Nuc (nucleus colony), which is a small hive of bees already in a frame that you insert into your Langstroth or Top Bar hive depending on which type you specify in your order. You can catch your own swarm, a natural colony that is already organized and living in the wild but this is definitely not recommended for beginning beekeepers.

You should order bees from an Apiary in the autumn months or in early winter. Nearly every Apiary ships their bees during the first months of the year although some wait until April or May.

Ask local beekeeping associations and clubs about ordering bees and pick their brains while you're at it. You'll rarely find competitive or protective attitudes because nearly all beekeepers are happy to support each others' efforts. They know that bees are good for the earth and the more we have the healthier our environment will be. You may even find beekeepers that have surplus bees they are willing to sell you. This is a good way to buy bees because you can be assured of their good health and vibrancy.

Chapter 5. Feeding Your Bees

Yes, you do have to feed your bees! Bees normally eat their own honey; the combs are created and filled specifically to sustain the bees, particularly during the winter. If you leave enough honey for the bees after you harvest you won't have to worry about feeding them. However, if it has been a season of poor nectar flow and there isn't much honey you'll have to supplement their diet. You'll know if they are short on sustenance if you can pick up your hive easily since a colony needs to store at least 50 pounds of honey to make it through the winter. If the honey production has fallen short of the bees' needs you can feed them sugar syrup, pollen patties, fondant, sugar candy which you can make yourself, or you can buy commercially made bee food.

You will need to feed your bees periodically throughout the winter if you don't leave them enough honey to sustain them. Check frequently to see if they need food or if the hives need maintenance.

Many experienced beekeepers feed their bees discolored or otherwise unmarketable honey during the winter. Bear in mind that nothing is as good for bees as the product they make for themselves.

Chapter 6. Choosing Your Honey

The flavor of honey is influenced by the plants from which bees get the nectar used to make it. There are a few hundred kinds of honey in the U.S., each with a different taste depending on where the bees gathered their nectar.

Beekeepers can choose how their honey will taste by positioning their hives close to the plants that influence the taste. Alfalfa, cotton, sunflowers, pumpkins, and other agricultural crops can produce honey with tastes ranging from very sweet (red clover) to a strong honey with an aftertaste of molasses (buckwheat). If the bees frequent Canola flowers the honey will be peppery.

Wildflowers produce very distinctive flavors, too. The much-hated dandelion helps to produce honey with a wonderful aroma and a strong flavor while honey made from Goldenrod nectar is richer with a more delicate odor. If there are many wildflower varieties near your hive, your honey will be quite interesting!

Honey is also made from the nectar of the blossoms of fruit trees, almond trees, basswood, acacia, poplar, willow, pine, and others. Fruit tree nectar is fickle, depending on the crop that year; it can be influenced by temperature, rainfall, and soil conditions. Some very interesting honey can be gleaned from bees that frequent apple or avocado trees, olive trees, orange or mango trees.

If you do not live within "bee distance" of the blossoms you would like, you can ask a property owner if you can position your hives on or close to his or her property. Since bees are critical to pollination most people will wholeheartedly agree to the arrangement.

Chapter 7. Harvesting The Honey

When about 80% of the comb is covered with wax the honey is ready to be harvested. Be sure to wear your protective gear and have your smoker ready. Have an area ready that the bees cannot access, such as a room that is tightly sealed or screened, since bees will try to take the honey once they recover from the effects of the smoke and realize a comb is gone.

Come up to the hive from behind, using the smoker to distribute smoke around the hive's entrance. Remove the top of the hive and quickly blow smoke into the opening so that the bees move into the lower reaches of the hive then remove the inner cover. This is where a small hive tool/crowbar may come in handy as the bees tend to saturate the cover with propolis. Use a bee brush to remove any remaining bees from the frame then take the frame inside for extraction or set it aside while you remove others.

Once you have the frames you want, use an uncapping knife or another implement to remove the seals from the comb. You can even use an ordinary kitchen knife, two of them if you want the work to be easier. Heat a knife in hot water and use it to cut off the cap. When the knife cools, replace it with the other that has been in the hot water and place the used one there to re-heat. Once the combs are uncapped you can then put the honey in a honey extractor and spin the honey out, straining it through layers of cheesecloth. Your honey is now ready to bottle.

You can invest in an electric extractor or you can get an inexpensive model that requires you to crank a handle to spin the "pot". The idea is to remove the honey using centrifugal force. The type of extractor you get depends on how big your honey-making operation is and how much effort you want to expend.

Once the honey is extracted you can replace the frames in the hive; be sure to have your smoker ready and wear your protective gear. Remember to leave enough honey in the hives for winter feeding if you want to raise your colony in as natural an environment as possible. Otherwise, you can harvest the honey and leave substitute food in its place that will help sustain them throughout the winter.

Take care when harvesting the honey not to damage the combs. A properly handled comb can be used repeatedly and last for up to twenty years if you treat it gently.

Chapter 8. Keeping Your Bees Safe

Bees have natural enemies that can decimate your colony. Hornets, wasps, and yellow jackets will all attack your colony unless you take steps to keep them away. Make sure there is no place to for water to accumulate and stand after a rain, or leaf piles that can retain water. Secure garbage cans tightly so that wasps and hornets are not attracted by the sugars.

You can buy an imitation wasp nest at any big box store or independent garden center. Wasps, yellow jackets, and hornets will avoid an area where a nest is already established; when they see the fake nest they will stay at least 20 feet away. If you want to save money, simply blow up a brown paper bag and tie it off then hang it in a convenient location to deter these insects.

You can also make a trap for the pests without harming your bees. Use a mixture of 2 tablespoons sugar and a cup each of vinegar, fruit juice, and water heating until the sugar is dissolved. Let it cool then pour it into a large plastic soda bottle, leaving the cap off. Hang the bottle near any ripening fruit or hang some fruit near it if you have no fruit trees. The wasps will fly into the bottle but can't fly out. The vinegar keeps your bees away from the trap.

When autumn approaches you'll need your smoker once more so that you can install mouse guards on the hives. Mice are fond of raiding hives for food when the weather turns cold. Mice also carry parasites and mites that can sicken your bees and destroy your colony so keeping them out of the hives is important. During the warmer weather the entrance is guarded by bees but when the weather turns cold it's up to you to protect the hive. You can buy a commercial mouse guard of stainless steel for a few dollars or make your own out of angle iron or a similar metal with bee-sized holes drilled into it. If you make your own, be very certain (usually through close observation) that the bees can easily come and go. If the bees can't move in and out of the hive, even in winter, the colony will die.

If you have harsh winters in your area you'll want to prepare the hive by covering it with a heavy plastic bag over R19 insulation. Staple the bag along the bottom of the hive so that the bees won't die of the cold. Be very sure to leave the entrance of the hive accessible so that the bees have access to the outside as well as fresh air.

Chapter 9. Dealing With Disease and Pests in The Hive

Varroe mites are the most common bane of beekeepers, tiny oval mites that appear on the thorax area of the bees. The mites lay their eggs alongside the bees' eggs and develop along with the young bees. They feed on the fluids in adult as well as pupal and larval bees and carry a virus that causes deformed wings. Varroe mites have been known to destroy wild colonies and are a huge problem for domestic beekeepers. A hive is particularly vulnerable while they prepare for winter or if the nectar crop in summer is not sufficient. There are chemicals that can destroy the mites or more natural methods such as dusting with powdered sugar to encourage cleaning behavior, thus dislodging the mites. Another method is a VMCE (varroa mite control entrance) that rubs the mites off the bees as they enter or leave their hive.

Tracheal mites can't be seen because of their size and because they settle in a bee's trachea (windpipe), choking them. You can guess if there are tracheal mites in the hive if you see workers on the ground outside the hive; they crawl out in an attempt to breathe and otherwise would be inside attending to their duties. These mites can be controlled with menthol crystals in the hives or sugar/vegetable patties, any of which can be left safely in the hive all year.

American Foulbrood, or AFB, is a bacterial disease that is often caused by used equipment; the spores of the bacteria can exist in a state of dormancy for years. AFB can destroy your hive by killing the pupae. If AFB is advanced in the hive you'll be able to see sunken or perforated caps. AFB is so virulent that most hives are burned to protect other colonies. Treating your hive regularly with Terramycin might prevent AFB. You should also avoid used hives or equipment. European

Foulbrood is less common but kills the pupae before they are capped; EFB responds to the same preventative measures as AFB.

Nosema is a disease that infects a bee's intestinal tract. If you see fecal matter on the front of the hive, your bees are likely infected with Nosema. If you notice signs of this disease you can feed the bees Fumadil B in sugar syrup to help them recover. It also helps to increase air flow throughout the hive.

The Small Hive Beetle (originally from Africa) infest hives and slime and pollute the combs. They grow outside the hive so the best way to prevent infestation is to mound diatomaceous earth outside the hive. This "earth" is actually sedimentary rock that crumbles easily, tearing the beetle's surfaces so that they die of dehydration.

Wax Moths are pests that don't directly attack your bees but eat the wax that the bees make for the honeycomb. The honey will be contaminated, the comb destroyed, and often the bee larvae perish due to this insect. Wax moths will die in cold temperatures so are not common in Canada or the northern areas of the U.S. If you do detect wax moths you can get rid of them by scraping the combs and the bees will replace them. Usually, the bees will take care of these pests by themselves.

There are many more fungi, bacteria, mites, and insects that can wreak havoc on your hive but don't get discouraged. If you keep your hive in good shape and take preventative measures with the hive and the area surrounding it, you can have a healthy colony.

Chapter 10. Care of The Queen Bee

The queen is literally the life of the hive, producing every bee in it for two or so years of her life. Therefore, you should have a healthy young queen with good genetic material for a quality colony. You can insure the quality of the queen by choosing a reputable breeder. If you already have a colony that needs a new queen you can buy queen cells, larvae that will emerge a few days after being introduced into the hive. A mated queen is also an option and will start laying her eggs soon after she is established in the hive. Queens generally cost about $20-$25 each. Many beekeepers raise queens as a hobby and you may find such an entrepreneur through your local beekeeping association.

A queen can lay more than 2,000 eggs a day, providing workers for the hive. The more workers you have, the more honey will be produced. Be particularly careful when you are inspecting the hive that you don't damage the queen by inadvertently crushing her or damaging her legs.

You don't have to do much to take care of the queen other than making sure the hive is healthy and secure. Since the queen is not able to care for herself, attendant bees follow her everywhere to carry away her waste material, groom her, and feed her. If there is anything wrong with the queen she will produce a pheromone that alerts the entire hive of her distress and the attendant bees will see that she has what she needs.

Chapter 11. The Advantages of Beekeeping

Beekeeping is a fun hobby that can provide honey for your family or become a small enterprise to supplement your income. There are several advantages to keeping bee hives:

1. There are no complex technology requirements
2. Low investment
3. Requires very little room
4. No age limit, anyone can do it
5. Bees pollinate, contributing to a healthy ecosystem
6. Enjoy your own honey or trade/sell it

Although it does take some regular maintenance, bees generally take care of themselves as long as you make that the hive is structurally sound and protected from predators.

Thank You Page

I want to personally thank you for reading my book. I hope you found information in this book useful and I would be very grateful if you could leave your honest review about this book. I certainly want to thank you in advance for doing this.

www.ingramcontent.com/pod-product-compliance
Lightning Source LLC
Chambersburg PA
CBHW070521290526
45790CB00003B/1262